Miriam Halahmy was born in London in 1952. She was writing before she could read, 'in my head', and taught herself to read before starting school. Miriam has written and published short stories, articles, poetry and a novel. She has reviewed books for the *TLS*, *Jewish Chronicle*, *Jewish Quarterly* and *Everywoman* magazine.

A teacher of children with Special Needs for twenty-five years, she now enjoys painting, gentle exercise, travel and leading Creative Writing workshops. She is a member of the Highgate Poetry Society.

At the heart of her inspiration are family life and her identity as a Jewish woman. Miriam lives in Golders Green with her husband and their son and daughter – round the corner from their favourite bagel shop.

By the same author

Stir Crazy, Hub Editions, 1994, second edition, 1999
Secret Territory, a novel, Citron Press, 1999

Cutting Pomegranates

Miriam Halahmy

Published 2003 by David Paul
29 Redston Road, London N8 7HL
Tel. 020 8347 4857

www.davidpaulbooks.com

Some of these poems have been previously published in *Staple*, *Envoi*, the *Daily Express*, *Kites*, *Shofar*, and the anthology of Anglo-Jewish women poets, *The Dybbuk of Delight*. *Pomegranate* first appeared in *Stir Crazy*.

Text copyright © 2003 Miriam Halahmy.
Photographs of sculpture copyright © 2003 Oded Halahmy.

Miriam Halahmy asserts the moral right to be identified as the author of this work.

All rights reserved.

This book is sold subject to the condition that it shall not, by way of trade or otherwise, be lent, resold, hired out, or otherwise circulated without the publisher's prior consent in any form of binding or cover other than that in which it is published and without similar condition, including this condition, being imposed on the subsequent purchaser.

No part of this book may be reproduced, stored in a retrieval system, or transmitted, in any form or by any means, electronic, mechanical, photocopying, recording or otherwise, without the prior permission of the publisher.

Printed in Malta by Interprint Ltd.

Cover: from a photograph by Oded Halahmy.

Cover and text design, typesetting and production management by Will Shaman

wshaman@lineone.net

Set in 11 on 14pt Galliard.

ISBN 0-9540542-2-9

Publication of *Cutting Pomegranates* was made possible in part by the generous support of The Oded Halahmy Foundation for the Arts.

The Foundation, based in New York, is a non-profit cultural organisation created to fund original artistic expression of peace and hope by Jews and Arabs in the United States, the Middle East, and around the world.

In loving memory of my parents
Daphne Hyams Berk and Benny Berk

And wherefore have ye made us to come up out of Egypt, to bring us unto this evil place? it is no place of seed, or of figs, or of vines, or of pomegranates;

Numbers XX.5

Contents

I
Total eclipse	3
Washing apples	4
Builder's tea	5
Grown up	6
Packing up	7
My uncle	8
November 1991, Golders Green	9
Cheating on me	10

II
Beyond the courtyard	13
His place	15
Cutting pomegranates	17
Pomegranate	19
Loving	21
Haiku	23
Miriam's Song	24

III
Visiting Jack	27
Judentransport 3	29
Medical file	30
Noah's raven	31
Tasks and monsters	32
surviving	33
Exposed	34

IV
Portrait of an Old Boy	37
In the English lesson	38
Write about desire	39
Soft landings	40
Insecure in L.A.	41
Impressions out west	42

V
winter	45
March	46
Before midnight	47
Coping	48
Angel	49

VI
Summer drive	53
On Coniston Water	54
Hell's Angel Wrinkly	55
A poem for my father	56
Database	58
Getting acclimatised	59
Landing: July 1997	60

Oded Halahmy

'For me, the sensuous, red round pomegranates are around me all year long. I have them in my kitchen, my home and studio in many kinds of shapes, colours and materials: real dried pomegranates and ones in plaster, bronze, aluminium, silver and gold. They are my intimate art objects.'

The Sculpture

12	*Blue Party*	1976–82. Painted aluminium. H15′ W16′ D6′6″ (4.6 x 4.9 x 2m). Collection: The Aldrich Museum of Contemporary Art, Ridgefield, CT.
14	*Sky Window*	1973. Painted aluminium. H100″ W90″ D84 (2.54 x 2.29 x 2.18m). Collection: Lynn and Jeffrey Slutsky, Nevele Country Club, Ellenville, New York.
18	*Large and Round*	1964. Bronze cast. H34½″ W11½″ D10″ (88 x 29 x 25cm).
20	*Sky Moon Pom*	1997. Bronze cast. H35″ W23″ D8″ (89 x 58 x 20cm).
22	*Babylonian River Banks*	1989. Bronze cast. H96″ W49″ D17½″ (2.44 x 1.24 x 0.44m).

I

Total eclipse

We are so old in that minute
cave dwellers
without sun, hope
tumbled onto a planet strange
umbilical cut
our bodies painted black
absence of colour, light, heat.

We are naked
equal with the birds
God may call our name
we may respond
our minds scrambled in disbelief.

Then light returns swifter than dawn
I see my son
looking like my son
and the Earth
looking like the Earth
Tears dry on my skin.

Miriam Halahmy

Washing apples

Like Mandela casting his vote, I smile
and peel Cape stickers from green apples,
reel back years of vigil, marches,
taking my small son to sign.

He knows now why I said
at street stalls, in supermarkets, not those, or those
why it was never just an apple.

Builder's tea

Take one mug, thick white ceramic
mouthside chipped in a ragged V
drop in a teabag, Tesco value
cover with three heaped spoons
boiled water, full fat milk

set down on splintered plank, '2 be 4'
ringed with countless refills
watch as brisk March wind
dumps brick dust, hard core, sharp sand
onto the mud brown surface

retrieve cup, drained to the base,
handle smeared in multi-lube oil, wet cement
place with relief in dishwasher
re-start computer, open document, set up file,
sharp tap on patio door, 'Any chance of a cuppa, missus?'

Miriam Halahmy

Grown up

Don't cut her nails, hear her read
hold her hand at crossings, trim her fringe
zip her coat, choose friends, birthday presents,
don't dice her food, count her savings
fill her party bags, mix her cakes, decipher labels
check hot drinks with fingertip,

Don't read her diary, dictate letters, tiptoe in the night
switch off sockets, pretend we don't make love
kiss her in public, hide disinfectants, sleeping tablets, death
remind her to say thank you
don't take her temperature, she slides it expertly
onto heatpads,

Don't stop risks on roller skates, other people's trees,
check her breathing, feel her forehead, cover her at night,
don't sit on my hands, watch clocks,
as body slick in self defence suit,
black leggings, trainers size 1,
she turns the corner,
don't panic when she comes back late,
full of story, drunks avoided, cars shooting lights,
she is grown, almost ten, she decides.

Packing up

Into my box
I will put his first step
on legs unsteady as skittles.
I will put his scent
still freshsweet at fourteen
hair thick like mine
cut sport short to keep the eye steady, clear.

Into my box
I will put his confidences
on dark car journeys home from McDonald's
his sister tucked up in bed.

Into my box
I will put his height
arms round my shoulders, a teenage boyfriend,
his phone call from boarding school,
'In tennis group 4, playing for County.'
I will put his dreams
of groundshots sliced down the line,
Adidas sponsors, Centre Court cheers.

Into my box
I will put my tears now he's gone
close the lid,
wrap round a pale cord
severed red at the end.

Miriam Halahmy

My uncle

Curator of family knowledge
he researched, turned up on doorsteps of light year
distant cousins, not always welcomed in.
White-haired elder, deferred to, served first
he blessed the wine on Shabbos
taught the kids to sprinkle salt on bread.

Sometimes, tired of his moan
the convoluted drone of detail
I took a gap, did not phone for weeks
then missed him, table empty,
my mother's brother, her cadence
hinted in his voice.

We treasured scarce moments
humour like a sparkler here and gone
and tantalising visions
'My father made a cassock for the Pope
in Madame Tussaud's,'
this, weeks before he died.
My niece drinks it in
reminds us of names we scramble for.
I groom her to take over our baton.

November 1991, Golders Green

Windows misted to the frame
she sleeps, Alice in Wonderland duvet
tucked to the chin.

As if under water
fingers open, one by one.
The March Hare rolls his eyes.

Boots, military tight,
fog horn in the dark,
map street routes forward.

I lift the curtain
wipe fear like a white hole on glass
insinuate myself in shadow.

Voices swollen with power
bomber jackets, shaved hair,
'Sieg Heil, Sieg Heil, fucking Jew.'

Miriam Halahmy

Cheating on me

Here comes August
old prostitute
flowers faded in your red-dye hair

strut your green stuff
along days already crisp edged
nights dark before ten.

All through parched June
classroom stiff with tired bodies
I dream of holiday

cheer myself hoarse at sports day
comfort the losers.
I wave my girl off to camp

then it's my turn
August
air laced with your carbon cocktail.

As we shave short the lawn
lock up, head for the hills
sun angle shifts;

in see-through vest
you tease us
long-limbed shadow of winter.

The next group of seven poems are inspired by the life and work of my brother-in-law, Oded Halahmy, an Iraqi Jew who lives and sculpts in New York.

Miriam Halahmy

Beyond the courtyard

'If we lived in Baghdad
I would cast your sculptures in gold.'
Like the sun on bleached rooftops
where afternoon air shimmers, mirage high
calls of pigeon keepers circle, dive, regroup.

Eyes to the sky, breath tight in lungs,
you release your plum, your darling
rehearsed for weeks.
Beyond bird cages, where shadows gather
a maid fills water jars,
ice-cold by nightfall.
You will sleep with your brothers under stars
huge as the birds you train.

In your dreams the courtyard hums.
Women flow in and out,
constant as the river,
pile pita on benches,
hands steeped in flour,
shape *sambousaq* stuffed with walnuts,
closed with a thumb,
stuffed with dates, sealed with a key,
marked like a coded secret.

The gate swings open, you are gone,
beyond desert river, flying across English skies, Canadian snow
to breakdance with children of the Apple.
On city streets rhythms rise to skyscrapers,
sculpt rich blue light, throw shadows onto wood floor
where you have come to rest, dance,
break the limit of standard space.

Miriam Halahmy

His place

In his place
he puts bronze
soft when hot
moulded in movement
ready to bend line, space.

In his place
he puts colour
sun yellow, earth brown, clay red
silver hand flat, stamped against evil eye.
He will put Sight, Sky Window, Embrace
arms upward into blue.

In his place
he bellydances
drumbeat steady
kanoon, violin,
note longer than a breath
a thousand people cheer.

In his place
he sits between rivers
in flood across fields
black silt layered in spring.
He slices watermelon, hugeblown heads
juice pouring like fountains
into eager mouths of fishermen.

He leads his mother into his place
she shapes *kubeh, baqlawa, halqun*
mixes yellow pickle, cauliflower, carrot.
She pours oil on *humus*
cracks seeds; sunflower, pumpkin, melon
roasted on saffron rice.

Miriam Halahmy

He will capture in jars
scent of mint, cardomon, Old Baghdad
pigeons in cages on sunswept roofs
colour of sculpture, of light, of earth.

In his place
under palm trees
he sings with his hands
dances before wood
creates space, balances thought, casts desire.

Cutting pomegranates

My father quartered them with the bread knife
an old enemy, gripped me in its cunning
certain it would slip, spill blood
red as the juice on our skins.

We learnt with skill to bite hard
ease out each firm sweet seed,
ignore bitter stab of skin on tongue,
outback kids testing out terrain.

Sometimes I refused,
hating harsh kickbacks, only to envy brothers
thick shell flat against lips,
eyes mocking, bright dribble of promise on their chins.

Pomegranate

Breast heavy, this queen of Babylon;
beside water her tree stands tall
redsweet seeds bunch hard
bitter yellow membrane intact

With her round, fat, warm body
balanced in my palm, skin on skin
she is heavy
hot belly Babylon woman.

Miriam Halahmy

Loving

We made a Sukkah
nailed string corner to corner,
criss-crossed spider web suspended under sky.

Paper-cut bananas crayoned yellow
jostled with cardboard apples,
cereal packet adverts chopped in half.

Fresh carrots swung between pears,
precarious on noosed stalks
determined to work free.

Pomegranates, puffed cheek
crown poised, skin ready to burst
filled with promise, perfect.

Split open, you separate each seed
peel away yellow bitter shell
brimfill our bowls,

as fingers roll seed from membrane
fill your daughter's beautiful mouth
open lips purple with juice.

When the Messiah comes
our Sukkah no longer needed
I will cherish these lovegifts,

dried in a bowl,
remember your hands
hairs interlaced with lovelines.

Haiku

Pomegranate song,
lips in flower by river
I will bring my love.

A nightingale sings
in the pomegranate tree,
love springs before death.

I will pluck gently
with hands softened in sweet juice
seeds light as the stars.

Wear your crown tonight
abundant dreams spill from you
like oil on your skin.

Miriam's song

Afterwards
when she had towelled down
her tunic soaked with seaspray
torn a hunk of flatbread
from her lover's back
why not start a song
bring timbrels to shake desert air
watch bodies float
like pomegranates split open
seeds scattered on the water.

Voice high as a pyramid
peak knitted in whiteblown cloud
she would have a lot to say
how horse, rider hit the sea,
their arrogance locked in salt.

It would have been good to follow her
gather *manna*, heads bent together
whisper at night in charmed circles
reach the Promised Land, arm in arm
a rabble of giggling, dark tanned slave girls
scent of freedom on our skin.

III

Visiting Jack

I change lanes, thunder past a dirty lorry,
mentally check reminder list;
pockets empty, money for snacks,
handkerchief, did I forget I.D.?
Sweat breaks under my T-shirt,
I say nothing, we are already tense,
me about the sniffer dogs, body search,
Jack's wife about his current state of mind.

In the visitor centre, bright, pleasant
children busy with toys, we eat sandwiches.
'Like a holiday camp,' I murmur.
On familiar ground, she nods, sips her tea.
Suddenly it's time, a rush to the door,
she hates the endless queues.
We are slammed in, locked through
led up stairs, the children skipping ahead.
I produce my I.D., no dogs,
a search, fully clothed, and we are free.

They sit on regulation red chairs,
we hug and sit on blue chairs
his face relaxed today.
'Who does your ironing, Jack?' she quips,
the men sport pressed shirts, blue jeans.
A couple opposite embrace.
Jack nods, 'Both musicians, I borrow his guitar.'
Musicians, so why? But no-one asks that here.
We pump him about rules,
Why can't we send stamps?
'It's currency like tobacco, and…you know.'
He winks, I know, the absent sniffer dogs.

Miriam Halahmy

No appeal allowed,
banged up from five
he washes in his cell, listens to the radio,
pegs out socks, writes thousands of words.
All letters in and out are read,
his daughter not cleared to visit yet, includes,
'Dear Correspondence Officer, when can I see my Dad?'
scribbles pet names on the envelope.

Over 130 days he has built a plane,
painted a miniature chess set
filled endless files with notes.
'I'll need a lorry to get my stuff home,' he says.
I promise him one, anything,
rendered powerless on the blue chair.

Judenstransport 3: Paris, June 22nd 1942

For Great-Uncle Louis Silberklang (died Auschwitz, July 23rd 1942)

Part of my blood lies there
perhaps my smile
the way I slouch when tired
our DNA threads the years;

I open the letter guilelessly
stare through tears at his death
camp number 41253
shut my mind to those four weeks

dragged back to Poland, his birthplace
the papers sweat in my hand
tattered form photocopied grey
Berlin ticked in thick important pencil

I take the dictionary
hungry for each word
it falls open at *machtkampf*
struggle for power, masculine

search back for *dringend*, priority
sofort vorlegen, present immediately.
Urgent work shovelling 1000 Jews east.

Miriam Halahmy

Medical file

Postnasal drip, electrocardiograph
his teeth in a jar in Moscow.
Only one testicle
recorded by prison doctor, Munich
lost the other, perhaps in France.

As it happens, neither needed
relaxed only with his dog.
All Nazi top brass watched Blondi's tricks.
As Goebbels poisoned his children
was consumed with fear,
Did cyanide work for alsatians?

At Treblinka guards kept a zoo
to protect fauna in the nearby forest.

Noah's raven

Send the swallow,
brainless bird
plenty more where she came from!

Send the dove,
adrift in that dangerous storm
more rain and sky than ocean.

I'm an Eco-warrior
I cleanse the earth
hoover up all that stinking carrion
if I die, ravens will be extinct.

Send a thrush, blue tit, blackbird
orange beak to light the way
not me, ask what's her name
the wife, she'll understand.

Miriam Halahmy

Tasks and monsters

On automatic pilot I rose
brushed teeth, attended work
sorted washing

ignored warning light
fuel indicator
until, circuit failure imminent

I stopped, stayed home
stared at walls
telephone on answer mode.

Outside neighbours stalked,
the paper shop
an impossible journey.

Too tired to pair socks, flick t.v channels
dust became my friend
neglected plants sagged in disappointment.

Friends pressed round me
a wounded soldier, determined,
but prone to sink in potholes deep with mud.

In dreams, scree sloped peaks loomed
too difficult to descend,
the fearsome Loabbus,
jaws clenched to my legs.

And always my class asking why?
Where are you? We miss you.
                We miss you.

surviving

pine branch broken in the great storm
rules a charcoal line on winter sky

leafless it holds a dark memory
seared by wind intent on splitting wood

pinned to the earth
we log the same horizon

hungry for succulent new shoots
our hearts beat as pulsars in the night

Exposed

Coming out in a hot flush
coming out of love
coming out the boyfriend, your son's.

Coming out Tory, dyslexic
deaf in one ear, arachnophobic
coming out a computer date
coming out bulimic, wardrobe stuffed with crisps.

Coming out on Sabbath, whatever the neighbours
coming out 40, a murderer
fat, a fan of *Crossroads*
coming out a Lottery winner, in front of the family.

Coming out bald, coming out naked,
coming out black, mum or dad white
coming out poor, epileptic
coming out traditional.

Coming out with cancer
coming out without A*s
coming out white-horned
racist
Holocaust denier.

IV

Portrait of an Old Boy

(C. school. Sept '93 – Jan '95)

He has hung his grimy blazer
cuffs turned down twice, one final time
his last day unmarked, midweek
on corridors scuffed with Year 8 boots

he did not make basketball or chess team
hair shorn flat, small bald patch off centre
scar from a baby accident, head first pram to gutter
he was not light, bright enough to score

in reading class one dirty stub finger
pushed words on pages dense with incomprehension
mystery without foothold, language partitioned lessons
walled him in, ramparts skimmed with oil

he has gone to Tottenham, training not for cup final
but kebabs, greasedripped, impaled deep as desire
he will resume his education on someone else's patch
unknown, face wary, learn how to serve
wipe tables, listen for his heartbeat

Miriam Halahmy

In the English lesson

We read the Iron Man
made masks of blue and silver
stood tree tall
limbs swung in measured motion

like crabs on beach sand
we moved hand to headlamp eye
red softens into white
lights up the darkest corner

from the clifftop's broken edge
we swoop seagull swift
abandon one lost ear
reclaim the sea and poetry

the Thought-Fox roams our classroom
cold nose tipping folders
delicate search for scent
in the widening deepening green

we sigh for him, breath held
pen poised, clock ticking down to break
adrift in the lonely wood
a trail appears to lead us home.

Write about desire

'I want to be a big boy
a policeman, a goalkeeper.
I want a best friend,
Arsenal supporter, very tall, good at jokes.'

He passes me a photo
drip straggles his right hand,
transfusion day, grey sweatshirt, jeans
he is more defined out of uniform.

I ask about happiness.
'I am always happy,' he smiles
through yellow teeth, calcium leached
backbone already thin.

Slight body flutters down corridors.
Kitbags swung like concrete pendulums
he's learnt to dodge
determined gait points forward.

At night in bed
feed tube settled into stomach
he lies awake, logs digital bleep
knows he has survived twelve years.

In class he grits his teeth,
refuses to admit pain
afraid we will remove school,
his only benchmark.

We hover anxious, roles confused
teacher, helper, mother, nurse
he buries deep his strongest desire
to grow old like a big boy.

Miriam Halahmy

Soft landings

Mummy takes me, we go on the bus
I'm allowed sweets after.

The lady opens the door, 'Hello Mikey,'
I run and jump in the sand pit.

The lady says, 'Draw a picture Mikey,'
I draw a big blanket.

I like soft sand, bouncy blankets,
squashy pillows on my bed with teddy.

Daddy said, 'Get up on the window ledge
look at all the cars far below.'

Daddy held me tight by my legs
then I was cold, my T-shirt fell down.

Daddy held me by the ankle
my head was dizzy round and round.

Mummy screamed, Daddy shouted
people looked up with funny faces.

Daddy shouted, 'Don't leave me,' Mummy screamed
Daddy shouted, 'Promise or I'll let go.'

Daddy shouted, Mummy screamed
I was let go of, down, down, down, to the blanket.

Insecure in L.A.

I sleep with shoes fingertip close
ear cocked for earthquake bang
plates smashed together.

Outside El Nino rules
mudslides in the canyons
rain pours on streets
void of take-away litter, dog shit,
buffed only by soft-soled joggers.

In the morning, at ease
the kids full of waffles
we press buttons, set alarms
raise the garage door, release car lock
glide effortlessly from house to tarmac
no wind in our face.

At the museum my son jumps out,
loiters by a house.
'Wires run under there,' he points.
'Don't step on the grass, alarms go off.'

It's not natural movement they fear.
On lawns nail-scissor neat,
a warning, '*Armed response.*'

Impressions out west

Los Angeles spreads its wings
resistance paved over, interior plundered deep
names reveal old links, San Gabriel Mountains, El Segundo
  beach
Spanish is back, illegals swarm border fences
hawk nachos, mind children, shovel leaves

Everyone has an earthquake story
split foundations, swimming pools cracked dry.
Driven past rebuilt malls, we hurry over flyovers
car park pillars double back in agony

No-one talks of leaving
in Johnny Rockets juice drips from inch thick hamburgers
juke box pumps out Elvis
outside palm trees feather a blue rich sky
the sun, a satin peach, rides alone

V

winter

my son's head falls back
he flicks t.v. channels
tennis muscle gone
weight soaked away like water into sand

outside February grips coats to bodies
pale without the sun
I keep him indoors
safe beneath my gaze

close my ears to specialist
watch him fade
speak in brisk tones as he talks
of cutting it all away

hope comes in single grains
hepatitis B, tuberculosis
like a mantra
malaria, lupus, sarcoid

Angel of Death appears
to claim our first born
syringe of blood
smeared above his bed cannot cloak him

cancer breathes in corridors
removes hair, muscle, like trophies
turns my bowel to liquid
horizon into void

eyes remote, he rolls under blanket
I would change places now
without backward glance
give him my thirty years

March

Quarter of this year gone
his skin so sore
permits only finger touch
we wait;
at bedside, in day room
littered with old videos, car magazines
popcorn scuffed into carpet.

In the hospital shop I stand
rigid, mind on overload
stare at crisp packets
cannot choose.
Winter hangs heavy
a barrier riveted before us.

My son grips my arm
hauls himself from bed to wheelchair
I push him down corridors
remember buggy days
swing, slide, baby food.
Did I mix it wrong?
Has it returned,
cell structure imprinted
ingredients ill measured?

Before midnight

Surgeon's knife
is the border
crushed lymph node under glass
nothing definite
except his skin, bluewhite, needle marked
a fiver for each tally of ten,
his goal, twenty quid
mine, to take him home.

*We walked up mountains year on year
Snowden, Pen y Ghent,
he hauled me from thigh deep bog
carried all the food.
When he spat into wind
moisture flew back in my face
tattooed deep my skin.*

Monitor bleeps red, feed tube drips life
into stomach shrunken small.
Chest constricted I surface now and then
take a half lung of air
every cell of me waits, on hold.

Coping

Print his initials, ESH Bed 8
food labelled for the fridge
start a rubbish bag
refold paper
line up cartons with bendy straws
his throat closed, stomach on strike
produce a Kinder egg
like a TV mum
insist he eats both halves
dust CDs, set up washbasin
Harley Davidson deodorant
anti-acne face wash
wish his eyes would lighten
pick up socks
straighten sheets
take out plates full with lunch, dinner
refuse leaflets, helpline numbers
say my prayers
say them again
wish someone would save me

Angel

In Jerusalem
they prayed for you
lifted up eyes
pressed notes into the Cotel
prised open the Book of Life
said your name at the gates
Eliahu
said it again

Kikuchi came down
sat on your shoulder
bodyguard, soulmate
blew away fear
threw open the window
life streamed in.

Cotel: Wailing Wall. *Kikuchi:* A benign inflammation of the lymph system which mimics Hodgkins Disease.

VI

Summer drive

Lincolnshire,
hay stacked swiss roll neat
fields straight to the sky.

They know their ditches here
pull aside, wait patiently
I slither past breath held tight.

In Louth I brush a woman's arm.
Almost too late, call my apology
just as she says hers.

In London we just shove
road rage through the day.

Miriam Halahmy

On Coniston Water

I cast my line
into smug, smooth water
fishing weights skim down to where he lies
nudged by pike, the ancient Arctic char,

fastest man on earth
until Bluebird arced
in graceful flight
tossed him out like driftwood.

He waits now, head flatback, eyes dim
The Old Man of Coniston
dreams of movement faster than light
across oceans flecked with bird flight.

Hell's Angel Wrinkly

He offered me a ride on his Harley Davidson
feet forward, eyes skimming tarmac
pony tail streaked with grey

But I wasn't into risks, kids still small
hands held tight at crossings
fragile bodies strapped to seat belts

Careless now, I wave them off
one day bus passes, Oxford Street.
Back home, marooned, I cannot map intention.

I went, rarely sent a postcard home,
my mother cheered me on.
Dad still grabbed my hand at kerbsides
in my twenties.

Miriam Halahmy

A poem for my father
1921–1997

He has dates now
and I his music,
jazz breaks lazy round our house,
my son rings home
voice choked, broken
by Ellington on the radio.
Each first time is like this
no consolation after death.

Fluent in Yiddish, French
my father spoke just English,
dissected the world with logic
an expert on all that gripped him.
After his death we sorted tools, tapes,
notebooks filled with diagrams,
drawn in pencils
sharpened to precariousness.

Only faced with my mother's dementia
did he look lost, exposed.
Each morning he dressed her crisply clean
pinned on a different brooch,
never mind incontinence,
her silence, the way the head fell forward.
When she died he said,
'Thought I'd keep her going another year.'

His warmth heated households,
children, animals, reached for his lap,
behind him a Hackney childhood
frozen boys waiting for his apple core,
he in a suit, their feet bare.
At 17 he knew how to split atoms,
read it in a journal,
was searched out in '46 to lecture on the Bomb.
Everyone's father,
when he died
comforting the bereaved was a full time job.

Database

The nurses call him Joseph,
his birth name.
Like Pavlov's dogs we conform
ask for Joseph on the telephone.

He has his father's lips, Polish purple.
Grandpa wore pink shirts, silk ties,
Benny prefers sweaters.
He takes a 'small' now
and I, in middle-age spread
no longer fit his woolspun warmth.

Delinquent cells milk his lifejuice,
feet swollen, drain clamped against his lung.
Evening morphine kicks in. He drifts
fingers play across hospital blanket,
thumb on space bar, he taps keyboard
spreadsheet, formulae.

He gives us copies of his will
like graduation certificates
talks house prices
how to split inheritance when he dies
only love left to keep me warm.

Getting acclimatised

Have worked out the best toilet,
learnt to ignore signs.
Found Lift Bank B,
correct stairs down, nearest telephone.

Reclaimed an old school bag,
strap wrenched from nylon stitching,
for dirty washing, messages abroad,
Kleenex tissues, mansize.

Have decided on best corner shop
with citrus pressed juice,
grapes he may nibble,
nut chocolate for visiting grandchildren.

Have learnt to say firmly, Daughter
before quizzical frowns, cutting telephone tones,
to demand, criticise, kow-tow
before God's own profession
the magic makers,
who decide his next bowel movement,
body shift, cell type.

Have tried to choose when to visit,
when to take a break,
when to offer my arm down the ward.
Have learnt to deal with
hair loss, false connections,
imagined phone call in the night.

Miriam Halahmy

Landing: July 1997

On Yogi Rock
he rests his head
heartbeat in the stars,
constellations familiar
as his own backyard.

In Martian air
lungs on shutdown,
he sends us messages
of red run canal, fossil ribbed,
his universe complete.

We played cards last night
first time since,
arranged our hands as he insisted,
red card, black card, trumps at the end,
memorised every trick,
as he remembered each word read,
spoken, reflected.

Last hour
brain already shrunk
he spoke only of Mars
knew which path to take
death ignored.